Belmont

THE RIDGEWAY, MILL HILL

ET·VIRTUTEM·ET·MUSAS

LEARNING RESOURCES
CENTRE

Telephone: 020 8906 7270

EYEWITNESS
DISASTER
EARTHQUAKES!

HELEN DWYER

FRANKLIN WATTS
LONDON • SYDNEY

First published in 2010 by Franklin Watts

Franklin Watts
338 Euston Road
London NW1 3BH

Franklin Watts Australia
Level 17/207 Kent Street, Sydney, NSW 2000

Produced by Arcturus Publishing Limited,
26/27 Bickels Yard, 151–153 Bermondsey Street, London SE1 3HA

Planned and produced by Discovery Books Ltd., 2 College Street, Ludlow, Shropshire, SY8 1AN www.discoverybooks.net
Managing editor: Rachel Tisdale
Editor: Helen Dwyer
Designer: sprout.uk.com limited
Illustrators: Keith Williams, sprout.uk.com limited, (pages, 4, 8 and 9), Stefan Chabluk (page 10)
Picture researcher: Tamsin Osler

Photo acknowledgements: Corbis: 11 (Zhou Chao/epa), 14 (Bettmann), 16 (Craig Aurness), 18 (Roger Ressmeyer), 19 (Jim Sugar), 25 (Jeremy Horner), 27 (Reuters/Simon Kwong), 29 (China Daily/Reuters). FEMA: 24 (Casey Deshong). Getty Images: cover (Koichi Kamoshida), 5 (Joe Raedie/Staff), 6 (Adek Berry/AFP), 7 (Sankei Archive), 12 (Warrick Page), 13 (Paula Bronstein), 15 (Ernesto Benavides/AFP), 20 (Sankei Archive), 21 (Johnson Liu/AFP), 22 (Vincenzo Pinto/AFP), 23 (Franco Origlia). Istockphoto.com: 28 (Guillermo Montesinos). Wikimedia: 17 (H D Chadwick).

Cover Picture: Rescue workers at work in Nagaoka, Japan, following a series of powerful earthquakes that rocked northern Japan.

Sources
http://www.fordham.edu/halsall/pgc.asp?page=mod/1755lisbonquake.html page 4
http://www.peruviantimes.com/yungay-1970-2009-remembering-the-tragedy-of-the-earthquake/313073 page 7
http://www.hsv.com/genlintr/newmadrd/accnt1.htm page 9
http://news.bbc.co.uk/nolpda/ukfs_news/hi/newsid_7423000/7423870.stm page 11
http://news.bbc.co.uk/1/low/world/south_asia/4327882.stm page 12
http://news.bbc.co.uk/1/hi/world/south_asia/4347374.stm page 12
http://news.bbc.co.uk/1/hi/talking_point/6949537.stm page 15
http://www.sfmuseum.org/1906/ew1.html page 17
http://www.sfmuseum.net/hist2/presidio.html page 18
http://www.paulzilla.org/japanese/quakkurt.htm page 20
http://www.www.archive.inquirer.net/view.php?db=0&story_id=20806 page 21
http://news.bbc.co.uk/1/hi/world/europe/7985248.stm page 22
http://news.bbc.co.uk/1/hi/world/europe/7987362.stm page 22
http://www.bbc.co.uk/dna/h2g2/A2309276 page 25
http://news.bbc.co.uk/1/low/world/asia-pacific/6215991.stm page 27
http://www.sciencedaily.com/releases/2004/12/041219182609.htm page 28

A CIP catalogue record for this publication is available from the British Library.

Dewey classification number: 363.3'495

ISBN 9781445100586

Printed in China

Franklin Watts is a division of Hachette Children's Books, an Hachette UK Company.
www.hachette.co.uk

CONTENTS

WHAT IS AN EARTHQUAKE?

Earthquakes take place all the time. Every year, half a million quakes shake our planet's surface. But only about a fifth of these quakes are felt by us humans – the rest can only be detected by scientific equipment.

An earthquake is a movement in the ground. It is caused by events taking place inside the earth's solid upper layer. This layer consists of all of the **crust** and the top part of the **mantle** that lies below it. This solid layer is broken up into several large sections, called **tectonic plates**, which move around very, very slowly above the hotter, more liquid part of the mantle.

'In a moment I was [woken by] a most horrid crash . . . The house I was in shook with such violence, that the upper storeys immediately fell . . . the walls continued rocking to and fro . . . opening in several places; large stones falling down on every side from the cracks.'

Charles Davy, survivor of the Lisbon earthquake, 1755.

Colliding tectonic plates

Tectonic plates travel in different directions. As they move past, under or over each other, their edges can become stuck together. Eventually the pressure exerted by the moving blocks is so great that they break free. The energy that is released moves away in all directions like waves or ripples on a pond. These ripples are called **seismic waves**. They cause the shaking and moving of the ground that people call an earthquake.

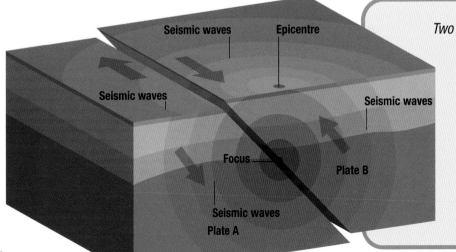

Seismic waves   Epicentre

Seismic waves

Seismic waves

Focus

Plate B

Seismic waves
Plate A

Two tectonic plates that had been locked together break free from each other, creating seismic (shock) waves underground. The place where the movement begins is called the focus. The arrows show the plates moving in different directions, both vertically and horizontally.

Focus and epicentre

An earthquake begins in the rocks below the surface of the earth. The place where it begins is known as the **focus**. The depth of the focus differs with every earthquake – from just below the surface to about 700 kilometres deep. The point on the surface directly above the focus is called the **epicentre**.

A series of earthquakes

A powerful earthquake may be followed by weaker **aftershocks** as the earth's crust adjusts after the main quake. In contrast, a series of small earthquakes may occur before a bigger one.

In January 2010 an earthquake on the Caribbean island of Haiti destroyed countless buildings and killed many thousands of people in and around the capital, Port-au-Prince.

EARTHQUAKE STORIES

Before people knew what caused earthquakes they tried to explain them in stories. Many of these tales involve animals. In Siberia (north-eastern Asia), people thought that the earth rested on a sled pulled by dogs that were infested with fleas. Whenever a dog stopped to scratch itself, the earth shook. In other stories, animals held up the earth: in Japan it was a catfish; in India it was either elephants or snakes; and in Mongolia it was a giant, twitching frog. When the animal moved, the earth shook. Native peoples in California thought that the earth was being pulled apart by huge turtles.

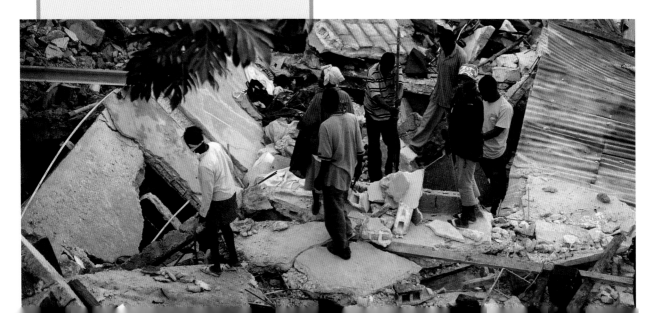

THE DANGERS OF EARTHQUAKES

Earthquakes rank with floods, famines and tropical storms as the most dangerous of natural disasters. In the 21st century, almost half a million people have died as a result of earthquakes.

An earthquake is most dangerous and destructive if it occurs near the surface of the earth. Places closest to the epicentre suffer the most damage. The damage also depends on how easily the seismic waves move through the rocks and land features.

Extra dangers

Earthquakes can trigger other dangerous natural events. The ground may break apart, leaving gaps several metres wide. When this happens, large structures such as bridges and dams may be destroyed.

The shaking can even change the soil, making it flow for a short while like a liquid. When this happens, buildings may sink into the soil or tilt over. In hilly areas, quakes can trigger **landslides**, which may wipe out whole villages and towns.

Deadly waves

Most dangerous of all, earthquakes in the seabed can trigger shock waves in the water, called **tsunamis**. These travel at great speeds for hundreds or thousands of kilometres across oceans and can cause massive destruction in coastal areas.

In Pariaman, Indonesia, the earthquake in October 2009 caused many landslides. Here only a narrow band of houses remains standing between two landslides.

THE DESTRUCTION OF YUNGAY

In 1970 an undersea earthquake off the coast of Peru, South America, brought disaster to the Andes mountains. The shaking dislodged a mountain **glacier**, which carried rocks, mud, snow and ice down the mountainside. This landslide struck the town of Yungay three minutes later. Most of the 25,000 townspeople were buried or crushed. Only 350 people survived, most of them children at a circus. They were saved by a clown, who led them up a hill to safety.

'I could see a giant wave of grey mud about 60 metres high . . . The sky went dark because of all the dust, mostly from all the destroyed homes.'

Mateo Casaverde, survivor of the Yungay landslide, 1970.

Collapsing structures

In many earthquakes, most injuries are caused by the failure of man-made structures. Poorly designed or flimsy buildings may collapse. Electrical power lines and gas and water pipes may break. As a result, people are left without shelter, power and clean water. Gas that leaks out of broken pipes is especially dangerous because it can **ignite** and cause fires. If water supplies are also cut there may be no water to fight these fires.

Fires rage out of control, the day after an earthquake struck Kobe, Japan, in 1995. Gas leaks started many of the fires, and older wooden houses burned quickly.

EARTHQUAKE ZONES

Nearly all earthquakes occur in places close to where tectonic plates meet each other. People in those areas have to be aware that an earthquake could strike at any time.

Tectonic plates can collide in a variety of ways but all these collisions cause earthquakes. There are two types of plates, oceanic (under the ocean) and continental (under the land). Oceanic plates are **denser** than continental plates.

This world map shows the main tectonic plates. The arrows show the direction of movement.

Sinking plates

Sometimes an oceanic plate is **subducted** (sinks) under a continental plate or under another oceanic plate. For example, the massive Pacific Plate is slowly moving north-westwards. As it moves it sinks under the North American Plate.

Collisions on land

When continental plates collide, both are of similar weight, so the rocks along the boundary are forced upward and form mountains. Sometimes – as along the San Andreas **Fault** in California – two plates slide horizontally past each other in different directions or at different speeds.

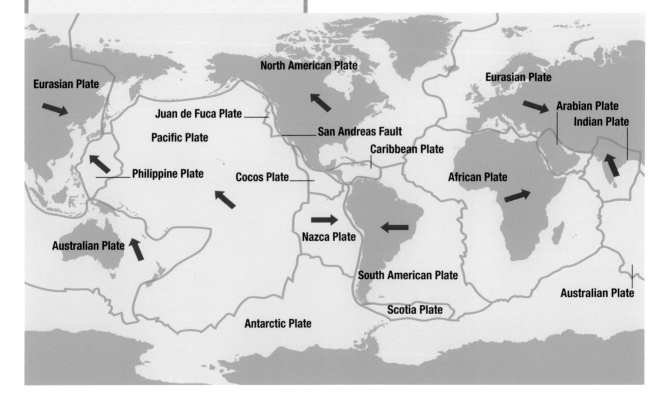

'We [felt] an earthquake, accompanied by a very awful noise [like] distant thunder . . . The screams of the affrighted inhabitants running to and fro . . . the cries of the fowls and beasts of every species, the cracking of trees falling . . . formed a scene truly horrible.'

Eliza Bryan, survivor of the 1811–1812 earthquakes in New Madrid, Missouri, United States.

Far from the edges

Occasionally, earthquakes occur in weak areas of the earth's crust far from tectonic plate edges. In 1811 and 1812 four major earthquakes – later known as the New Madrid earthquakes – took place in the US states of Arkansas and Missouri.

Every few years a minor quake strikes in Britain. In April 2007 the county of Kent was hit by a small earthquake, which damaged hundreds of buildings and was felt across the English Channel in France.

*An oceanic tectonic plate slides under a continental plate. The arrows show the direction of movement. As the plate sinks, earthquakes occur and land on the continental plate is pushed up to form mountains. The sinking plate eventually melts, creating **magma**, which may erupt as a volcano.*

AMAZING ESCAPE

Buried alive – twice

In 1976 an earthquake in Tangshan, China, killed 240,000 people. One miner, Alatanbagen Taoqi, was buried under **rubble** for ten days before he was rescued. Thirty-two years later an earthquake struck the Sichuan area and 60-year-old Taoqi was buried again, this time in an office building. A few hours later rescuers dug him out, still alive. He was the only survivor in the whole building.

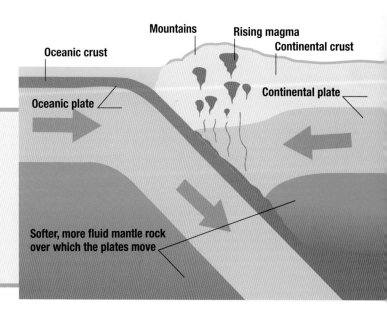

Mountains

Rising magma

Oceanic crust

Continental crust

Oceanic plate

Continental plate

Softer, more fluid mantle rock over which the plates move

CONTINENTS COLLIDE

Between 40 and 50 million years ago the Indian Plate collided with the Eurasian Plate. It was the climax of a journey that began about 150 million years before, when India was an island off the coast of Australia, thousands of kilometres from Asia.

Creating the Himalayas

About 200 million years ago the Indian Plate began to move northwards at a speed of about nine centimetres every year. When it struck the massive Eurasian continent, the rocks at the edges of both tectonic plates were pushed upwards. These rocks very slowly formed the Himalaya mountains, which stretch for nearly 3,000 kilometres along the border between India, Nepal and China. Some of the mountains, including Everest, are now more than nine kilometres high.

India continues to move northwards, pressing further into Asia. As a result the Himalayas are still rising by about one centimetre every year and the mountainous region of Tibet, in China, is pushing parts of Asia eastwards.

Stresses and quakes

These movements of the Indian Plate cause massive earthquakes every few years in the region. In the 21st century there have already been disastrous earthquakes in Pakistan, India, Central Asia and China. In May 2008 an earthquake in Sichuan, China, killed about 90,000 people and left five million homeless.

The collision between India and the rest of Eurasia creates not only the vast Himalaya mountain range but also causes constant earthquakes. Recent quakes are marked on the map. They show that even areas far away from the plate boundary are affected.

RACE AGAINST TIME

The 2008 Sichuan earthquake triggered landslides which dammed many rivers, creating new lakes. Scientists realized that one new dam in the Jianjiang River would soon burst and send a 20-metre-high wall of rocks, soil and water down the valley towards the large city of Mianyang. Something had to be done quickly.

A decision was made to release the water in a different direction. Explosives were used to create a new channel from the lake through the town of Beichuan, which had already been evacuated after earthquake damage. Although the people of Beichuan had to move into new homes, more than a million people downstream in Mianyang were saved from a disastrous flood and landslide.

A soldier carries an elderly man on his back in the panic to get out of a town in Sichuan, China, in 2008. People feared that a flood of water upriver would burst through the dam of debris, or rubble, left by the earthquake.

'These dams are . . . weak, loose piles of debris, under huge pressure from the river water building up behind. One more aftershock could suddenly transform this. . . It would rush off downstream, bulldozing and burying everything in its path.'

Geologist Stephen Edwards.

'Each village has about 250 houses. All of them are destroyed.'

KASHMIR 8 OCTOBER 2005

Reporters and aid workers who rushed to the earthquake zone described the situation to people across the world.

'Almost every shop in the bazaar is destroyed, the goods . . . now strewn across the twisted mass of wreckage. Mosques are down . . . along with . . . hundreds of homes and also schools.'
Andrew North, reporter in Balakot.

'The road has been blocked by a landslide . . . beyond . . . are many villages. People have come from these small mountain villages carrying the injured on their shoulders, walking for hours. Each village has about 250 houses. All of them are destroyed.'
Dr Irfan Noor, Mansehra district.

The region of Kashmir is on the border between India and Pakistan. It also sits on the boundary between the Indian and Eurasian Plates. On 8 October 2005 a major earthquake occurred in Kashmir. About 75,000 people died as buildings collapsed on them. These victims included 18,000 children who were attending schools and colleges when the earthquake struck.

An apartment block in Islamabad, the capital of Pakistan, was completely destroyed by the earthquake.

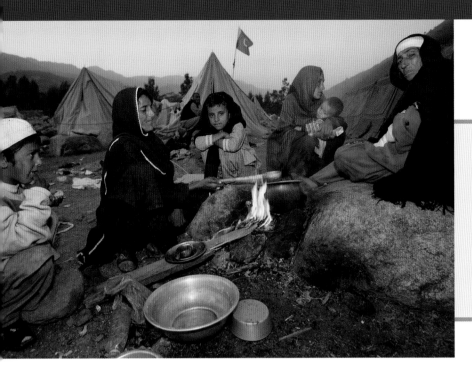

A homeless family cooks lentils over a fire in a city of tents in Balakot, Pakistan, where 90 per cent of homes were destroyed. Many of the homeless had to endure a winter without proper shelter.

Destruction in the mountains

Most of the damage was in remote mountain areas, where whole villages of mud-brick houses were destroyed. Help was slow in reaching survivors because landslides had blocked or destroyed many roads. More than a thousand aftershocks over the next three weeks also created difficulties for rescue teams.

A race against time

Yet another problem was that winter was beginning in Kashmir. Snow began to fall five days after the quake. It became a race against time to get homeless survivors to safety. Helicopters were used to fly in food, medicines, tents and blankets and to take out injured people and children who had lost their parents.

HELPING HANDS

The Pakistan government asked the North Atlantic Treaty Organization (NATO) for aid. NATO is a military **alliance** that was set up after World War II to defend its member countries in North America and western Europe from attack. It now includes Turkey and countries in eastern Europe.

NATO helicopters flew to mountain villages, delivering supplies and taking out the injured. NATO's engineers built shelters and repaired the damaged roads. Medical teams opened a temporary hospital to perform operations.

ALONG THE EASTERN PACIFIC

Many powerful earthquakes occur along the western coasts of North and South America as oceanic tectonic plates sink under continental plates.

Alaskan earthquakes

Along the coast of Alaska the Pacific Plate is subducting under the North American Plate. One of the biggest earthquakes ever recorded took place in Alaska in 1964. In some regions the shaking changed the structure of the soil so that it flowed like liquid. Buildings sank into the soil or tipped over. In other areas, landslides caused much of the damage.

The massive 1964 earthquake caused chaos in Anchorage, Alaska. Here sections of a road have collapsed and fallen six metres.

THE JUAN DE FUCA PLATE

The Juan de Fuca Plate is a small tectonic plate that sinks under the coast of North America. It has created the Cascade Range of volcanic mountains which stretch for 1,000 kilometres from Vancouver Island in Canada to northern California. Scientists fear that a big earthquake may occur here in the next 50 years, threatening the cities of Vancouver, Seattle, Portland and Victoria. In the meantime though, scientists are studying a series of hundreds of earthquakes which took place deep under the ocean in the middle of the Juan de Fuca Plate in 2008. **Marine** geologist Robert Dziak said: 'The fact that it's taking place in the middle of the plate . . . is puzzling. It's something worth keeping an eye on.'

Mexican earthquakes

Off the west coast of Central America, the oceanic Cocos Plate sinks under the lighter Caribbean Plate, creating an earthquake zone extending north into Mexico. In 1985 a disastrous quake off the Mexican coast killed thousands of people in Mexico City.

South American earthquakes

Almost the entire west coast of South America lies on the boundaries of the Nazca Plate and the South American Plate. The oceanic Nazca Plate moves eastwards by 3.7 centimetres every year. As it sinks under the continent it sets off earthquakes. The most recent major quake was in 2007 under the ocean near Peru.

'Everything was trembling – cars, the floor, walls – and there were odd lights that illuminated the sky many times. People were screaming and hugging because it was so long.'

'I have experienced tremors before, but never standing out in the street watching the trees swaying, light posts bending, and actually feeling the waves under my feet, with my knees shaking.'

Eyewitnesses to the 2007 earthquake in Peru.

The earthquake in Peru in 2007 disrupted water supplies in the town of Pisco. The local people had to collect drinking water from a tanker lorry.

THE SAN ANDREAS FAULT

Inland from the coast of California in the United States, the Pacific and North American Plates meet. The Pacific Plate is moving north-westwards, while the North American Plate moves south-eastwards. This boundary forms a 15-kilometre-deep, 1,300 kilometre-long **fracture** in the rocks, known as the San Andreas Fault.

A constant threat

As the two plates push past each other, movements along the fault are usually slow and steady, causing minor but frequent earthquakes. However, parts of the plates sometimes become stuck for many years, so pressure builds up. When the plates break free from one another, this pressure is released and big quakes occur.

San Francisco, 1906

In 1906 a large earthquake occurred on the San Andreas Fault. The city of San Francisco was badly hit and many buildings collapsed. The quake was followed by fires, which were caused by gas pipes and chimneys breaking, stoves overturning and electric cables touching each other. Four days later, when the fires were finally put out, 80 per cent of San Francisco had been destroyed, more than 3,000 people were dead and a quarter of a million people were homeless.

The spectacular San Andreas Fault is easy to see from the air. For millions of years two tectonic plates have slid past each other in opposite directions, creating mountain ranges and triggering earthquakes.

RAGING FIRES

In San Francisco in 1906, fires caused more destruction than the earthquake. The city's fire department had no water to fight the fires because water mains and the supply pipes from reservoirs had been broken. Some houses were blown up with dynamite to create gaps which the fire could not spread across. Unfortunately the explosions created even more fires. Then a navy officer arrived and ordered all the tugboats in the harbour to pump sea water out of the bay and feed it into the firefighters' hoses. At last the fire department was able to control the fires.

An area of San Francisco that was badly damaged in the 1906 earthquake and fire. Very few buildings were undamaged and many were simply rubble.

'Power and trolley [*tram*] lines snapped like threads. The ends of the power lines dropped to the pavement . . . writhing and hissing like reptiles. Brick and glass showered about me . . . Buildings crumbled like card houses . . . a second shock hit . . . I was thrown flat and the cobblestones danced like corn in a popper.'

Thomas Jefferson Chase, survivor of the San Francisco earthquake and fire, 1906.

'It was moving like a wave, just like water.'

SAN FRANCISCO, USA 17 OCTOBER 1989

Army Staff Sergeant David Langdon was at a baseball game in San Francisco when the earthquake occurred.

'The spooky part . . . was looking up in the stands, completely full . . . To see the slabs above the upper deck separate by feet and come back together, and watch the light stanchions [upright posts] sway left and right . . . about fifteen feet [4.5 metres] either way, it was a sight to behold . . . Then to look out to the field and just see it roll as if it were an ocean, because it was moving like a wave, just like water; waves and waves and waves.'

On 17 October 1989, a part of the San Andreas Fault which had been stuck since the 1906 San Francisco earthquake suddenly moved. The earthquake that followed lasted 15 seconds and caused severe damage in the San Francisco Bay area.

Empty roads

The quake struck at 5 pm, just as a professional baseball game between two local teams, the Oakland Athletics and the San Francisco Giants, was starting in San Francisco. Fortunately, many people had

This building in San Francisco sank into the soil because the earthquake changed the soil's structure and made it act like a liquid. The car is trapped underneath the third floor of the building.

The remains of the Cypress Freeway in West Oakland, where 42 people were killed when the top deck collapsed and crushed their cars.

left work early or stayed in town to watch the game on TV, so the roads were much emptier than usual. If the traffic had been as heavy as it normally was at that time of day, many more people would have been killed or injured.

Death and destruction

Most of the deaths and injuries occurred on a highway **viaduct** in West Oakland, where the top deck of the bridge collapsed onto the lower deck.

In Santa Cruz – near the earthquake's epicentre – many historic buildings collapsed and six people died. In San Francisco, multi-storey buildings in the Marina District were badly damaged and a section of the San Francisco – Oakland Bay Bridge collapsed.

LIQUID SOIL

In San Francisco the collapsed highway viaduct and the badly damaged Marina District were built on marshland. Both these areas were filled in with rubble, sand and dirt to make the ground firmer before construction began. However, the shaking during an earthquake makes the wet, unstable soil behave like a liquid. Buildings on solid rock are much less likely to collapse during an earthquake.

EASTERN ASIA AND THE PACIFIC PLATE

Several countries in eastern Asia – especially Japan, Taiwan and the Philippines – face the same problems as the western coasts of the Americas. They are located where continental and oceanic tectonic plates meet, so they are prone to frequent earthquakes.

The Kobe earthquake

The islands that make up Japan were created by plate boundary movements. In 1995 a powerful quake struck the region of Kobe in southern Japan, where two million people live. Many old houses collapsed because their wooden walls were badly damaged and could no longer support their heavy tiled roofs. The tiles fell, crushing the floors below. In contrast, modern buildings, which were designed to withstand earthquakes, suffered minimal damage.

'Roof tiles clogged the street. Dust filled the air. Smoke was rising. The smell of gas filled the world.'

Kurt Mundt, survivor of the earthquake in Kobe, Japan, 1995.

The force of the Kobe earthquake crumpled up this main road, which toppled on its side. Many roads and railways were badly damaged in the quake.

A block of flats in Wufeng tilts dangerously after the Taiwan earthquake in 1999, the most destructive earthquake on the island in more than 60 years. Since 1999, Taiwan has experienced several smaller earthquakes.

Taiwan disaster

The island of Taiwan is another earthquake disaster area. Quakes in Taiwan usually begin under the sea, but in 1999 the island was devastated by a quake that originated under the island. Fifty thousand homes were destroyed and 2,400 people died. In many areas the quake triggered landslides which crushed houses under tons of rock. The damage was so serious because Taiwan's cities are not built on solid rock. The ground consists of rocks and rubble that have fallen or been washed down from the mountains.

AMAZING ESCAPE

Miracle survivor

In 1990 an earthquake struck Baguio City in the Philippines. A 27-year-old physical fitness instructor named Pedrito Dy found himself trapped under rubble in the basement of a hotel which had collapsed. With no food to eat, Dy survived by dipping pieces of foam rubber into rain water that fell through the rubble. He even drank his own urine. Finally, after 15 days, rescuers spotted Dy's hand in the rubble and pulled him out, bruised but uninjured.

'I was hungry, thirsty and scared . . . I lost hope several times . . . I just waited for death to come . . . It was a miracle.'

Pedrito Dy, survivor of the Philippines earthquake, 1990.

'I was flung around like a rag doll.'

L'AQUILA, ITALY 6 APRIL 2009

Shaken survivors told reporters how they escaped from damaged buildings in the middle of the night.

'Everything fell, the plaster from the walls and all the furniture . . . the way to the stairs was blocked by a piece of furniture . . . When we eventually got out to the street . . . another terrible shock occurred. We thought we could be hit by the collapsing rooftops, by bricks and plaster.'
Vittorio Perfetto, in L'Aquila.

'The walls shook violently and I was flung around like a rag doll . . . I was able to escape through a stairwell that was crumbling as I ran down it. The rest of the village looked like a battlefield and was mostly destroyed. It looked like a massive bomb had gone off.'
Gabriel Kornel, in the village of San Gregorio near L'Aquila.

Italy in southern Europe is part of a very active and complicated earthquake zone. In April 2009, the country experienced its worst quake in nearly 30 years.

Trapped in bed

After two smaller earthquakes the day before, the main earthquake struck the city of L'Aquila and surrounding towns and villages in the middle of the night, when most people were in their homes in bed. Several buildings collapsed and thousands more were damaged. Rescue efforts to help trapped people were made more difficult by several minor aftershocks over the next few days. In all, more than 300 people died and 65,000 others saw their homes destroyed.

Italian fire service workers carry an injured victim on a stretcher out of a damaged building.

INADEQUATE BUILDINGS

After the quake, many Italians demanded to know why modern buildings – even ones that were supposed to be earthquake-proof – had collapsed or been badly damaged. One of these buildings was a new hospital. As its walls gave way, medical staff had to get the patients out and then treat the injured outdoors.

Experts said later that building standards were not enforced properly in Italy. They believed that the new hospital was poorly built. It should have been able to withstand a severe earthquake.

Why was the damage so bad?

The earthquake was very damaging for a number of reasons: the epicentre of the quake was very close to the surface – only ten kilometres underground; the city of L'Aquila was built on the unstable bed of an ancient lake which made the shaking stronger; and the city contained many buildings hundreds of years old that were not built to resist earthquakes.

L'Aquila is full of old, historic buildings. Many of them were destroyed or badly damaged.

UNDERSEA EARTHQUAKES AND TSUNAMIS

Tsunamis are giant ocean waves that are caused by the movements of earthquakes under the sea floor or by landslides that tumble into the sea. Tsunamis travel across oceans at speeds of up to 1,000 kph and may be more than 15 metres high when they reach land.

Long-distance travellers

Not surprisingly, these waves can cause enormous damage when they reach a shore. Earthquakes along the western coasts of the Americas – from Alaska to Chile – have caused tsunamis which travelled across the Pacific as far as Hawaii and Japan.

Destruction in Portugal

In 1755 an earthquake in the Atlantic Ocean to the west of Portugal destroyed many buildings in Lisbon, Portugal's capital city. Forty minutes later a tsunami swept over the harbour, through the city and up the River Tagus. The giant waves caused death and destruction along the southern coast of Portugal.

A Pacific Ocean tsunami struck Samoa and American Samoa in the South Pacific in September 2009. This is the badly damaged village of Leone in American Samoa.

'The ground shook . . . The buildings started to fall down. The only noise was tumbling masonry [stonework] and the screams of [people] trapped in the church . . . I could see the sea disappearing as if sucked down a hole. Then the ocean returned, all at once, taking with it the church . . . and the bridge.'

Report on the 1755 earthquake and tsunami from a priest in the Algarve region of Portugal.

A tsunami wave created by an earthquake under the Indian Ocean hits a holiday resort in Thailand in the 2004 disaster.

The 2004 Indian Ocean disaster

In 2004 a massive earthquake occurred under the Indian Ocean. It lasted for more than eight minutes and the movements in the seabed extended across 1,600 kilometres. The tsunamis which followed travelled as far as the coast of southern Africa. Altogether 230,000 people died in eleven countries around the Indian Ocean.

TSUNAMI WARNING?

Japanese **seismologists** are keen to find out what is happening under the oceans around Japan so that they will have some warning before earthquakes or tsunamis strike. Scientists are now boring holes in the sea floor near Japan to collect rock samples. These samples can be analyzed to show where the worst stresses are. Japanese scientists plan to run an undersea cable to this region so that data from scientific instruments can be sent back to Japan. The information collected may help to predict the next big earthquake and tsunami.

MEASURING AND PREDICTING QUAKES

The strength, or **magnitude**, of an earthquake is usually expressed in the moment magnitude scale, which is very similar to the earlier Richter scale. It grades an earthquake in numbers from one to ten. In this system, a magnitude 6 earthquake is ten times bigger than one of magnitude 5, which is ten times bigger than a magnitude 4 quake.

The easiest way to understand these numbers is to have an idea of the damage the quakes cause. For example, an earthquake that measures between 4 and 5 will make objects inside a house shake, but it will not damage the house; one that measures between 8 and 9 can cause serious damage for hundreds of kilometres around the epicentre.

Seismographs

Earthquake vibrations are detected and recorded by electronic instruments called **seismographs**. The measurements can tell scientists how far away the earthquake began and how powerful it was. Measurements taken by several seismographs in different places indicate where the earthquake began.

Detecting changes

Earthquake prediction is not very accurate, but scientists are constantly working to improve it. They measure gases and magnetic activity in the earth as well as stresses in rocks. They also study past earthquakes, looking for earthquake patterns that repeat themselves.

EARTHQUAKE STRENGTH

Magnitude	Description	Effects	Frequency
0–2.9	Micro	Usually not felt	Thousands every day
3.0–3.9	Minor	Often felt but rarely damaging	About 50,000 every year
4.0–4.9	Light	Objects in buildings shake or rattle	More than 6,000 every year
5.0–5.9	Moderate	Damage locally to poorly constructed buildings	About 800 every year
6.0–6.9	Strong	Slight damage to well-constructed buildings	About 120 every year
7.0–7.9	Major	Moderate damage to well-constructed buildings	About 18 every year
8.0–8.9	Great	Serious damage over hundreds of kilometres	About 1 every year
9.0–9.5	Great	Serious damage over thousands of kilometres	About 1 every 20 years

A seismologist at Taiwan's Central Weather Bureau points out the differences between two earthquakes that occurred on the island on the same day in 2001. The computer printout of the vibrations is called a **seismogram**.

SENSITIVE SNAKES

Scientists in China believe that snakes can be used to predict earthquakes because they behave strangely as long as five days before and as far as 120 kilometres away. The Chinese now study the behaviour of some captive snakes on video 24 hours a day, looking for signs that an earthquake is about to occur.

'Of all the creatures on the earth, snakes are perhaps the most sensitive to earthquakes. When an earthquake is about to occur, snakes will move out of their nests, even in winter . . . the snakes will even smash into walls while trying to escape.'

Jiang Weisong, Chinese earthquake scientist.

Scientists in Parkfield, California, United States, think that sensitive new instruments may be able to detect tiny changes in the rocks a few hours before an earthquake. That would be long enough to get people away from buildings and to alert the emergency services.

Clues in nature

Nature may also provide warnings of earthquakes. For centuries, sudden heat waves, brilliant lights in the sky and changes in water levels in lakes, ponds and wells have all been felt and seen before earthquakes. Animals seem to register natural changes better than humans do. In Tangshan, China, in 1976, people noticed that several species of animals became agitated before a major earthquake.

PREPARING FOR EARTHQUAKES

In an earthquake, most deaths and injuries occur when buildings collapse. Even in minor earthquakes, buildings are damaged.

Building design

Some older structures can withstand earthquakes quite well. Pyramid-shaped structures are very stable. Dry stone walls and timber-framed buildings can survive earthquakes because the separate parts can move slightly without the whole structure falling apart.

Architects now know a lot about designing buildings to resist earthquakes. Steel is used to strengthen concrete, stone and **mortar**. Another way of stabilizing buildings is to build in special structures called **dampers**, which absorb the shaking. If an earthquake shakes the foundations, the vibration does not affect the rest of the building.

'The world's exploding mega-cities have yet to experience a major earthquake, but it's only a matter of time before one or more occurs.'

Roger Bilham, seismologist.

Unstable ground

Perhaps the most important safety measure of all is to avoid building on unstable ground in earthquake zones. Wet ground, sandy soil, clay and rubble all transmit seismic waves very easily and even **amplify** them.

Torre Mayor in Mexico City (see box on page 29) is one of the most earthquake-resistant structures ever built. It is designed to cope with an earthquake of magnitude 8.5.

LESSONS FROM MEXICO CITY

In 1985 an earthquake under the Pacific Ocean caused the deaths of 10,000 people in Mexico City, 350 kilometres away. Many buildings collapsed in the centre of the city, which was built on an old lake bed, consisting of moist layers of sand, silt and clay. This type of ground vibrates strongly when an earthquake strikes.

Between 1999 and 2003 a 55-storey building called Torre Mayor was built on the old lake bed. Architects included lots of dampers in the design. These dampers absorb vibrations from quakes and prevent them shaking the structure. When a strong earthquake occurred in Mexico City in 2003, the people in the building did not even feel it.

Safety rules

However safe a building is, people still need to know how to act during an earthquake. The first thing to do is drop to the floor and cover yourself with something solid like a table. If this is not possible, sit against a wall away from windows and things that might fall on you.

If you are outdoors you must keep away from buildings, trees and electricity lines because they could fall on you. After a quake there may be minor aftershocks – or even a stronger quake – so you must stay alert.

School children take part in an earthquake practice exercise at a primary school in China. This will help them know what to do if a real earthquake strikes.

GLOSSARY

aftershock a smaller earthquake that follows a large earthquake

alliance an association of members with the same interests

amplify to make something stronger

crust the outermost solid layer of the earth, between 5 and 50 kilometres thick

damper something that absorbs shocks and vibrations

denser more solid

epicentre the point on the earth's surface directly above the place where an earthquake begins

fault large crack in the earth's rocks where the rocks have moved in different directions

focus the place where an earthquake begins

fracture a crack in the earth's rocks where stresses have made it break apart

geologist someone who studies the earth's rocks

glacier a slow-moving mass of ice which is formed from layers of crushed snow

ignite to begin burning

landslide a fast-moving mass of rocks and debris which rushes down a slope

magma liquid rock beneath the surface of the earth

magnitude a measurement of the amount of energy released by an earthquake

mantle the 3,000-kilometre-thick, mainly solid layer of the earth beneath the crust

marine relating to the sea

mortar the mixture of cement, sand and water that is placed between stones or bricks in buildings, to hold them together

rubble a large number of pieces of broken rocks of different sizes and shapes

seismic wave the vibrations that travel through the earth during an earthquake

seismogram a computer or paper record of an earthquake

seismograph an instrument that detects and records the strength and direction of earthquakes

seismologist someone who studies earthquakes

subducted describes what happens when one tectonic plate is pushed under another

tectonic plates the parts into which the earth's crust and upper mantle are broken up and which move around independently, creating earthquakes

tram a bus that runs on rails and is powered by electricity drawn from overhead wires

tsunami a sea wave caused by undersea earthquakes, volcanoes or landslides

viaduct a bridge that carries a road above a valley or an obstacle

FURTHER INFORMATION

Books

Blakes, *Earthquake (Go Facts: Natural Disasters)*, A & C Black Publishers Ltd., 2007

Ganeri, Anita, *Earth-shattering Earthquakes and Violent Volcanoes (Horrible Geography)*, Scholastic, 2006

Green, Jen, *Volcanoes and Earthquakes (Our Earth)*, Wayland, 2010

Jennings, Terry, *Earthquakes and Tsunamis (Amazing Planet Earth)*, Franklin Watts, 2009

Langley, Andrew, *Natural Disasters (Kingfisher Knowledge)*, Kingfisher Books Ltd., 2006

Oxlade, Chris, *Earthquakes and Volcanoes (Earth's Changing Landscape)*, Franklin Watts, 2006

Rae, Alison, *Earthquakes and Volcanoes (Looking at Landscapes)*, Evans Brothers Ltd., 2008

Rooney, Anne, *Earthquake (Our Angry Planet)*, Franklin Watts, 2009

Shone, Rob, *Earthquakes (Graphic Natural Disasters)*, Franklin Watts, 2010

Tanaka, Shelley, *Earthquake!: On a Peaceful Spring Morning, Disaster Strikes San Francisco (Day That Changed America)*, Madison Press Books, 2009

Van Rose, Susanna, *Volcanoes & Earthquakes*, DK Publishing, 2008

DVD

Natural Disasters. DK Eyewitness Books, 2009.

Websites

There are many websites that tell you about earthquakes. These are just some:

http://www.earthquake.usgs.gov/learning/kids/
Earthquakes for Kids has lots of animations as well as photo collections, project ideas and information on the most recent earthquakes.

http://www.science.nationalgeographic.com/science/earth/the-dynamic-earth/plate-tectonics-article.html
This National Geographic site includes information on the major earthquake in Turkey in 1999 and videos of earthquakes.

http://www.fema.gov/kids/quake.htm
This site shows which areas of the United States are most at risk from earthquakes and explains in detail the ways we measure earthquakes.

http://www.howstuffworks.com/earthquake.htm
How Stuff Works includes lots of information on how earthquakes work, including plate tectonics, seismology, prediction and lots of photos.

http://www.nature.nps.gov/geology/usgsnps/pltec/pltec1.html
This explanation of plate tectonics has lots of diagrams which look inside the earth and illustrate tectonic plate movements over time.

http://www.pbs.org/wnet/savageearth/earthquakes/index.html
This site focuses on plate tectonics, learning from earthquakes, prediction and building safety.

http://www.sfmuseum.org/1906/06.html
The Great Fire and Earthquake site from the Virtual Museum of the City of San Francisco contains lots of interesting eyewitness reports.

INDEX